TIM HERRERA

CRISIS COMMUNICATION PLANNING

Crisis Communication Planning

A Guide to Dealing with the Media during a Crisis

Tim Herrera

© 2014 Tim Herrera, Sacramento, California

All rights reserved. No part of this book may be reproduced or transmitted in any form or by any means without written permission from the author.

CRISIS COMMUNICATION PLANNING

Introduction	10
What is a crisis?	14
Plan in advance of a crisis	22
Create a crisis media management team	28
Develop a Strategic Communication Plan	34
Selecting a spokesperson	48
Put your spokesperson to work	56
Develop key messages	64
Determine the best channel of communications	70
Stick with what you know and be honest	80
Communications duties during a crisis	86
Who are your "interested parties"?	92
Immediate response duties checklist	98
What the media will ask about during crisis situations	...106
Crisis meeting agenda	...112
Professional help or do-it-yourself?	...116
Crisis management checklist	...124
Relax	...128
About the author	...130
Thank you!	...132
Other books by Tim	...134

CRISIS COMMUNICATION PLANNING

TIM HERRERA

There cannot be a crisis next week. My schedule is already full.
-Henry A. Kissinger

CRISIS COMMUNICATION PLANNING

TIM HERRERA

Introduction

  Bad stuff happens. And that bad stuff often happens when you least expect it and are least prepared. This book is about preparation and getting a plan in place to deal with the media in the event that bad stuff happens.

  If you run a company, an association of some kind, or lead a nonprofit organization, you probably have many plans in place to guide you in the event of something going wrong. You probably have a business plan, a blueprint to follow to help your group be successful. There is a good chance your group has all kinds of procedural manuals to help you navigate the tricky world of personnel. Hopefully, you have a plan in place in the event of an emergency such as an earthquake or fire, an evacuation plan.

  But do you have a plan in place to deal with media in the event of an emergency or some kind of crisis? Now you do. This book, *Crisis Communication Planning: A Guide to Dealing with the Media during a Crisis,* will help with your preparation process.

  It's true that we can never really plan for a crisis. We don't know when something bad might happen. However, we can plan to be prepared in the event of something going wrong because we need to be ready to react.

You will notice throughout this book that I am big on creating checklists. Keep in mind that – during slow times and hectic times – checklists can be our friends. Trust me when I say that checklists will be your friend during times of crisis when you have to work with the media.

After reading this book – and after you have collected all the tools and tricks you need – you will be properly prepared to work with the media during difficult times. It's just a matter of planning. That may seem oversimplified but preparation is the key to anything.

If you follow the advice in this book, you will find yourself ready to handle any crisis communication situation. Keep in mind that this isn't a textbook, although I guess it could be used as one and I wouldn't discourage any college or high school from buying this book in great volume for their students.

Crisis Communication Planning: A Guide to Dealing with the Media during a Crisis is a simple guide that will help you in your communication planning efforts.

Read on and enjoy!

Something good comes out of every crisis.
-Dave Pelzer

TIM HERRERA

What is a crisis?

As we get started, let's peer into the dictionary. Let's define what we should consider to be a crisis. What is the definition of that word?

-A turning point in the course of anything

-A decisive or crucial time

-A time of great danger or trouble, whose outcome decides whether possible bad consequences will follow.

"Crisis" has many definitions of different lengths and detail. Basically, a crisis is any situation which requires immediate and coordinated action that could have significant impact on the organization or its reputation. A crisis is an unexpected event or series of events that create a lot of uncertainty that can threaten your organization's goals.

During a crisis, your group's reputation and image have to be managed just as any other organizational asset. The role of the mass media – which includes social media - during crises has been a topic of discussion for a very long time. Criticism of how media handles itself dates back centuries. Thomas Jefferson once wrote: "The man who reads nothing at all is better educated than the man who reads nothing but newspapers." Many people still hold that type of mistrust today, although that mistrust goes beyond print and into electronic media.

During times of crisis, there is a great deal of uncertainty and fear. People turn on their televisions, or log onto the Internet or check their Smartphone, to get the latest information, analysis of the current circumstances, and to make sense of things. Most people look to the media to reduce uncertainty and fear by receiving what they believe to be accurate information.

There are several questions that are raised about this. First, is the information sources are providing journalists accurate? Sometimes CEOs and spokespeople publicly react too quickly, without having all the facts, or the right facts. This can compound the crisis. Also, are the journalists accurately reporting the information? This cannot be guaranteed during crisis situations. It's up to professional communicators to monitor the reporting and speak up when inaccuracies are reported.

The news business today moves at lightning speed. Many stories now are broken on blogs or websites rather than in the Sunday morning newspaper or the 11:00 p.m. news. The race by news organizations to be the first and the fastest to report a big story means that now, more than ever before, it is vitally important that the news sources – CEOs, Board Presidents, and other executives – learn how to react accurately, promptly and properly during crises.

Newspapers, news radio stations, 24-hour cable news operations and every other media outlet imaginable can have great impact, both negative and positive, on any given situation. A company cannot control how a news organization reports a story, but that organization can control how it interacts with a news organization and how it provides information.

During a crisis, an organization's future can hinge on how stakeholders perceive and react to how the company or organization handles a situation. Failing to communicate properly during a crisis is one of the biggest mistakes any organization can make.

By nature, humans don't really like to plan for crises. Basically, we don't want to plan for the possibility of bad things happening. However, the truth is that with acts of terrorism in our own country, with high profile incidents of workplace and school yard violence, it is important that you have some kind of plan in place no matter whether you are the owner of a medium-sized business or the operator of a small nonprofit organization.

The bottom line is that you need to learn how to deal with bad news. You need to know how to respond during a crisis.

Every business, every school, and every organization is required to have some kind of emergency evacuation plan in the event of some kind of crisis. For instance, companies practice fire drills. Employees know where to meet in the parking lot if the fire alarm goes off. But how many groups or organizations have a media crisis plan and practice it? The answer: very few.

Most of your big city law enforcement agencies frequently stage disaster drills and part of those drills includes handling the media. But most organizations do not have a media crisis plan, or if they do have some kind of disaster drill written down on paper that blueprint does not include how to deal with the media in the event of an emergency.

Think of a crisis media plan as being like an insurance policy; you don't really want to use it but when you do you are glad to have it. The difference between a media crisis plan and an insurance policy is that a plan will only cost you the time and effort it takes to put it together. You won't have to worry about rising premiums, that's for sure!

The best thing to do to prepare for a possible crisis is have a plan prepared and tucked away somewhere knowing that you will only pull it out of the drawer and blow the dust off it in case of emergencies.

Think of a crisis media plan like the jack in the trunk of a car; you only pull it out and use it in the event of a flat tire. It's the same with a crisis media plan; you only use it on rare occasions.

What types of crises are we talking about that could involve your organization? Here's a partial list of possibilities that could bring the media to your door:

- Accident/Death
- Crime
- Natural Disaster
- Employee misconduct
- Financial problems
- Protest
- Product recall

Again, this is just a partial list. Anything and everything else can happen that could be considered a crisis.

In our next section, we spend some time exploring the process of planning for a crisis. That won't jinx you and cause a crisis to happen, but it is good to be prepared.

TIM HERRERA

I like those crisis moments - if you're on top of it and don't get pulled under by panic and fear, it's a very bonding thing.
-Bill Pullman

TIM HERRERA

Plan in advance of a crisis

You first need to realize that you have to make your crisis communication plan simple and user-friendly. It can't be too long or complicated. Try to keep the steps and rules to a minimum. Realize that you cannot anticipate every possible emergency that could hit. It's a waste of your time and the time of your staff members and co-workers to try and craft crisis communications plans for every possible scenario you could face. Make your plan as general as possible so that you can adapt its use to various occasions.

Understand that the planning takes place long before there is any crisis. It is really difficult to develop any type of plan if you are creating one on the fly. It's like constructing a house without building plans – you never know what your end product is going to look like.

So, here we go with a helpful little checklist of things to keep in mind when you are creating a crisis media plan:

-Plan in advance for a crisis (which you are already doing!)

-Create a "crisis management" team that you can call into action quickly.

-Spell out what you want to accomplish

-Develop a strategic communications plan (we will discuss this later)

-Put your spokesperson to work (the one you should have already chosen)

- Develop key messages
- Determine the best channels of communications
- Stick with what you know
- Be honest and open
- Relax
- Determine who your "interested parties" are
- Develop an immediate response checklist
- Determine what the media will ask during a crisis
- Create a crisis meeting agenda
- Consider if you can handle the crisis yourself or if you need professional communications help

Here's a brief side note that's important to mention right now. Professional communications or public relations help might be **exactly what you need**. If that's the case, then seek the help. Just keep in mind that getting such help can be costly. Contracting with a professional communications firm can mean paying big bucks. If that firm assigns a junior executive to your account you can expect to pay at least $95 an hour to work on your project. An experienced account executive charges close to $150 an hour. BUT if they want to call in the big guns to handle your account – like a senior account executive – you can expect to be billed as much as $300 an hour. Check around but the rates are fairly standard in the communications business.

Basically, talk AIN'T cheap!

Keep in mind that hiring an expensive professional communications firm, PR agency or communications specialist to work for you or your cause does not necessarily guarantee that you will get better results than if you hired a less expensive company to do the work. But the opposite isn't necessarily true either. But, if you think the job is too big for you then seek professional help. It could be money well spent.

So, how does one actually prepare for something to go wrong? What I am saying is plan in the event that a crisis occurs but keep working as if no crisis will happen. You can't live in fear.

The point is to be ready to react in case you have to. Have something written down in a binder and make sure that key members of your staff know that there is a plan to follow in the event of a crisis where the media is involved.

Meet with staff periodically to review your plan so that everyone understands the proper protocol. You need to make sure that staff understands what steps your organization will take in the event that you have to enact your crisis media plan.

In our next section, we will discuss how to put together a crisis management team, who to place on that team and what duties they should assume. Planning involves detail and we are going to get detailed.

TIM HERRERA

A man has no more character than he can command in a time of crisis.
-Ralph W. Sockman

TIM HERRERA

Create a crisis media management team

Hopefully, your organization has safety plans in place in the event of an emergency. If there's a fire, earthquake or other kind of emergency, people need to know how to respond. People need to know who to contact and what to do in the event of an emergency or disaster. You should have a similar team in place for crisis media management. In fact, it is a really good idea to include dealing with the media in your overall emergency planning. Make that one facet of your emergency plan. This book will help with that.

If – heaven forbid – something bad happens and the media is descending on your organization, you need to have a plan in place by which you have people prepared to handle media requests, reporters at your location, calls from out of town journalists, or just about any other possibility.

Please keep in mind that the planning we are discussing here involves dealing with the media and managing the media during a crisis. If you need to develop an overall emergency response plan, which includes an Incident Management Team, then you should consider contacting a professional to help in that area.

NOTE: This book does not deal with developing a disaster response plan. That is a separate project that deserves your attention.

Regarding the developing of your plan for responding to the media during a crisis, one of the first things you should do is pick a handful of dependable staff members that you know you can trust to act responsibly during stressful moments. They need to be able to handle pressure and work well in a group. You also have to have faith that they can and will make responsible decisions.

Below is a list of the types of tasks to which you will need to assign people in the event of a crisis involving media coverage:

-Initial point of contact (The person taking media calls who will funnel messages to the Media relations lead – see below)

-Media relations lead (The person who will coordinate with the media and work with the spokesperson – see below)

-Spokesperson (The person who will be doing the talking with the media)

-Logistics (The person who will stage people, determine where to put media, "live" trucks, and stage news conferences.)

-Web/Social media lead (The person who will handle posting updates on your website and social media sites)

-Stakeholder liaison (The person who will be the conduit of information for specific groups such as clients, Board members, parents, sponsors. This part depends on the type of organization that you are and what you do)

-Legal counsel (The legal expert who handles all things legal, whether this is s staff attorney or outside counsel)

This is by no means a complete list. Depending on your situation and your organization, you might want to create different tasks. It all depends on the situation and on your available staff. However, it is really important in times of crisis that these duties are divvied up.

Assign separate tasks to team members. Some of them might deal with the press, others might handle inquiries from the general public or constituents, others might deal with facilities issues, food and water, or even traffic control. Meet with your Incident Management Team periodically just to make sure that they are prepared in the event of an emergency.

Depending on the size of your operation, you might want to consider creating or appointing some type of group designated with responding to emergencies. It is really important that you have some type of Incident Management Team that is designed to complement and enhance your media response plan.

This team should be comprised of staff members, personnel or dedicated volunteers who can be quickly called together to help you in time of need. Your designated communications spokesperson – if you have one - can work directly with the Incident Management Team to facilitate distribution of information. Without having some kind of team in place, your job of informing the general public will be much more difficult.

In our next section, we will dive deeper into the planning process.

TIM HERRERA

To effectively communicate, we must realize that we are all different in the way we perceive the world and use this understanding as a guide to our communication with others.
-Tony Robbins

TIM HERRERA

Develop a Strategic Communications Plan

This section is going to get a little labor intensive and urge you to think and contemplate a little more. In the next few pages, we are going to delve into planning some more. Earlier, we talked about planning for a crisis and in this section we are going to discuss developing a Strategic Communications Plan.

Does your agency or organization have such a plan? If not, this section will help you develop one. In many cases, these types of plans are centered on a specific issue or cause. For example, is your company about to release a new product? Is there some sort of major expansion around the corner? Are you launching a new outreach effort to connect with new stakeholders? If the answer is "yes" to any of these scenarios, then you will need a media plan to accompany these types of situations. You will need some type of map to help you navigate the process.

However, having a Strategic Communications Plan will help you in times of emergencies as well, provided you have the time to put these steps into action.

When you are in the beginning stages of crafting your Strategic Communications Plan, it is really important that you ask yourself some questions:

-What is the issue?

-What is the solution?

-Who can help you create change?

-Who needs to be mobilized?

These questions are germane whether you are working for a short term or a long term goal.

The great philosopher and Hall of fame baseball player Yogi Berra once said, "If you don't know where you are going, you are certain to end up somewhere else." That is true in life, and in communications. If you are planning to launch a fundraising campaign, a volunteer recruiting drive, or if you want to increase your customer base – and you are planning on implementing a communications component to get the word out– you really need to develop a strategic communications plan. If you are rapidly responding to a specific issue, you still need a plan.

Some companies, groups and governmental bodies like to have a procedural plan written out for media. It's good to have guidelines.

This is an opportunity to map out in detail exactly what you're involved with or facing. When formulating your communications plan it's good to ask yourself **"What's the issue?"** What we mean by "issue" is the topic of concern. What's got you all in a ruffle, or what are you hoping to get others all in a ruffle about? Sometimes seeing these things written down will help you make more sense of things.

Then you need to pose this question: **What's the solution?** This is usually the solution you'd most like to see. It's kind of like visualization, seeing the answer right before you. It's kind of like when we searched the back of the algebra book for answers to problems we struggled with while in school. We had the question, and then we read the answer in the back of the book. Then we figured out what to do to get to the right answer. In this case involving media management, have the answer to your problem figured out and work toward it. Think of it as reverse engineering.

Another question: **Who can help you create change?** In answering this question, you will actually come up with more than one list. First, you should put together a list of people you are trying to reach with your message. These people could be new customers, new members, or local politicians. The list can be limitless. Also put together a list of people that you feel might "represent well". These are people who could speak on your behalf or serve as solid references. (We'll get to the topic of selecting spokespeople later on in this book.)

Finding people who could "represent well" will come in extremely handy if you are putting together a task force or some kind of ad hoc committee. Finally, if you do not already have an established list of media contacts that can help circulate your message, then this is the time to start developing one.

Who needs to be mobilized? When putting together a media plan, think about which people or community leaders to recruit. Again, if you are assembling a task force or community group this is a useful list to have for many reasons.

It is also important that you develop a **central theme** for your project, like a mission statement but not as formal. Write one sentence stating "what this is all about" and follow that sentence.

For instance, let's say your goal is to recruit new members for your social organization. Make that your statement: "We want to recruit more members, increase our numbers and become more influential." Once you start building on a statement like that then your chances of success will increase.

Finally, identify the **"power holders"** in your community: community leaders, parents, students, teachers, legislators, state officials, business owners. These are the folks who are right in the center of your target's bulls-eye. Keep them in mind as you are directing your message toward them. This hold true whether or not you are facing a crisis situation.

So, what is strategic communications planning? It means what the name implies. Not only do you need to develop a plan, but you have to be strategic about it. Each aspect that you design has to have meaning. There has to be a reason behind each move that you make when developing your blueprint.

So, what is strategic communications planning? It means you as the leader of a small business, nonprofit organization or community group must use communications to create or strengthen connections with your key audiences. It's the development of a master plan. If you were planning a cross country road trip from San Francisco to Atlanta, would you travel without a trusty map, or a functional GPS system? I would not recommend it.

When developing a strategic communications plan, you are creating a flexible framework to identify your goals, audiences, methods of transmitting your message, and methods of evaluation.

Benjamin Franklin, founding father and currency face model, once said "By failing to prepare, you are preparing to fail." By developing your strategic communications plan, you are improving the chances that you will not fail in getting your message out.

Now, in the previous paragraph you might have noticed that I called this a "flexible framework." What do I mean by that? By that I mean few plans are perfect and go off without any complications. While developing your plan, you must be willing to make changes along the way if you notice that your initial strategy is not working.

You can lay out all of your challenges in front of you to see what roadblocks to steer around. Here is a listing of elements contained in a very basic strategic communications plan:

- Executive Summary
- Background
- Situation Analysis/SWOT
- Core Problem/Opportunity
- Goals and Objectives
- Key Publics and Messages
    - Message strategy to each
    - Recommended strategies
    - Recommended strategies for making presentation to media representatives
- Calendar

-Budget
-Evaluation – Course Re-direction?

Let's go into more detail about each one of these areas. This should give you a better idea of why each of these areas is important and why they rely on each other for support.

Executive Summary: In a clear and concise way, write an overview of your project. You want to sum up the key points of your plan for your readers who, in this case, would be people connected to your organization who might need to know about, or approve this plan. If anything, this executive summary would help keep you on track so that you don't lose focus. Executive summaries save readers time and help prepare them for the upcoming content and are sometimes called the most important part of any plan.

Background: This is a brief summary of the entire situation and why you need to develop this plan. Briefly describe the situation, and the players involved. A brief organizational history is good, but don't go as far back as the dawn of time.

Situation Analysis/SWOT: This is where you write a brief analysis of your situation. **SWOT** stands for Strengths, Weaknesses, Opportunities and Threats. This is a useful tool for any organization that wants to develop a deeper understanding of what to do in any decision-making situation. It is always a good idea to do your SWOT Analysis during a brainstorming session, so that you can get flooded with good examples. However, it is best to whittle your list down to a manageable number. The primary purpose of this analysis is to assemble a list of relevant aspects, and then search for answers to them. You can always do these in the form of a chart, like this:

Strengths	Weaknesses
1.	1.
2.	2.
3.	3.
4.	4.
5.	5.
Opportunities	**Threats**
1.	1.
2.	2.
3.	3.
4.	4.
5.	5.

Core Problem/Opportunity: I guess to be very direct; I would say that in this age of political correctness and overuse of cheery and positive words, that both "core problem" and "opportunity" are really the same thing. Some folks insist on using the word opportunity – or even challenge - instead of problem because they believe it is a more positive approach. To that I say, whatever makes you happy. However, whatever word you decide to use, take some time to sit down and really figure out your core problem/opportunity/challenge is. It is your main reason for developing this strategic communications plan. Don't just write a sentence or two. Really explore all angles of the problem/opportunity that you are facing. Explore all of the angles.

Goals and Objectives: These are not interchangeable words. Goals and objectives are different. Your goals are your general intentions. They are broad in nature. They are almost like intangibles. Objectives are narrow and more precise. While goals really cannot be validated or quantified, objectives can be validated and quantified. For example, let's say one of the main reasons you are developing a strategic communications plan is that you want to increase membership in your nonprofit organization. So, let's say that your GOAL would be "increase membership". Can that really be validated? Well, sort of. But can it be quantified? Not really. Now, let's say that your OBJECTIVE is to "increase group membership by 10-percent" by July of this year. Can you quantify that? Absolutely!

Why create lists of goals and objectives? It is good practice to create targets, both broad and specific. Every organization or group needs benchmarks to reach for and try to attain. You need to have goals and objectives.

Key Publics and Messages: This is where you make a list of the important people you are trying to reach with this strategic communications plan. I would recommend that you use the names of real people and not just generic ones like "politicians" or "millionaires." However, if this is an overarching plan, and the first time you are putting one together, go ahead and work in generalities. Attached with each name, compose a list of messages that you will use to reach out to each of them. The messages might be similar for each group. Also come up with a list of recommended strategies for getting these messages out to the people you are trying to reach. By that, I mean are you going to use an e-mail campaign, are you going to create posters and place them in your community, are you going to hold public forums? It is a really good idea to do these in list form like this:

>**Public:** Mayor Al Catraz
>**Message**: We need more stop signs near our local schools because people are driving too fast in school zones.
>**Strategy:** E-mails, postcards and phone calls. Hold community forums to discuss safety.

Calendar: When developing any kind of plan, whether short term or long range, you really need to know when things need to get done. You need to have it all written down.

Budget: It is really important that you put in writing how much money, if any, that you are willing and able to dedicate to this project. It is also really important that you stick to that number. It is okay to spend under the amount you set aside, but never spend over that amount.

Evaluation – It is always good that you evaluate any plan you create. Of course, you cannot evaluate something until you have done it. So in this section you should write out HOW you will evaluate your plan in order to determine if it worked or not. Figure out how you will determine if you have succeeded. This will provide you with an opportunity to redirect your course of action.

Now, if you have the means to hire a communications professional to do this for you, then I would suggest you do so. It would be money well spent. If you do not have the means, and that is why you bought and are reading this book, then go ahead and start planning. You will learn a great deal through this process. This will be your strategic communications plan that you created. There is a great deal of personal satisfaction that can come from that.

After reading this section you might be asking yourself, "How in the heck can be expected to develop an elaborate Strategic Communications Plan if I have the media breathing down my neck and I need to respond ASAP?"

Good question!

The answer is that you really can't create a detailed plan on the fly as things are happening around you. However, these steps in forming such a plan and the questions you need to answer while constructing it will help meet your needs.

Remember, having plans in writing will serve as useful guides.

Now, when you are in the midst of some kind of crisis and the press is asking questions, someone has to answer those questions. So, who will do the answering and how will they do it? That's what we will discuss in our next section.

TIM HERRERA

Half the world is composed of people who have something to say and can't, and the other half who have nothing to say and keep on saying it.
-Robert Frost

TIM HERRERA

Selecting a Spokesperson

The Merriam-Webster dictionary defines a spokesperson as "a person who speaks as the representative of another or others in a professional capacity." Pretty much every company, especially the large ones, has a spokesperson of some type. Some organizations have gone to great lengths to select the right person, while other groups just pick a warm body who can string a few coherent sentences together.

I would not recommend that second option and soon will explain further.

Interviews can be intimidating, even for those with media experience. A spokesperson must know how to articulate the "company line" for lack of a better phrase. Whoever is chosen as your spokesperson must know how to advance your organization's goals, viewpoints and objectives. The person chosen for this role has a lot of responsibility because the media's power cannot be ignored and sometimes you only get one shot and representing who you are and what you do. You have to get it right.

One of the first questions you might ask is "how important is it that we even think of having an official spokesperson? Is communications really that important?"

Well, communications is a big deal. Increased media visibility is driving the need for more and better communications, which is driving the need for good spokespeople to represent you and your group or organization.

So, how do you go about selecting a spokesperson and why should you select one in the first place? Let's answer the second question first. You need to select a spokesperson because you need one person to handle media inquiries and to make inquiries to the media.

You need one representative with whom the media, and eventually the public, can identify. You also don't want several people handling media inquiries because you want to speak with a consistent voice, and you don't want several people doing the same job. As we all know, the left hand and the right hand don't always communicate. It's important that you have stability in the communications area.

Now, there are several things to consider when selecting someone to serve as your group's spokesperson:

-That person must be articulate and well-spoken.

-That person must convey trust and credibility.

-He/she must appear to be genuine and sincere.

-A good spokesperson is good at thinking quickly on his/her feet.

-Even though you might be "the boss" your organization's spokesperson might not necessarily be YOU.

That last bullet may hurt your feelings, but you have to face the truth.

Perhaps you are a wonderful and personable leader with a brilliant business mind, but maybe you are not the right one to serve as the spokesperson. Take a good, hard look at yourself to determine if you can "represent well" if called upon to answer questions from the media.

Ask those who work for you, or with you, if they feel that you could handle the task. Don't get upset if they respond to you honestly and you don't like what they are telling you. Insist that they be honest, and tell you if you are not the right guy for the job.

If they tell you they believe someone else should speak for the group, then accept their judgment gracefully and find the right person who will represent the organization well. You will still be heavily involved in the crafting of the "company message." You just won't be the person who delivers that message.

Not everyone can be a spokesperson. If you are going to go through the effort to find someone, one of the best things you can do (if you have the money) is have that person professionally trained. If you have the money to do it, it is money well spent. It only takes a simple Google search – or a search on the search engine of your choice – to find companies that train spokespeople. It is money well spent, if you have the money to spend.

There are plenty of good, reputable companies out there that specialize in media training. If you don't have the money for professional training then there are some simple and inexpensive ways to practice and prepare yourself.

- Make sure staff knows that you (or your designated spokesperson) will be handling all calls from the media. Tell them to NOT answer press questions themselves.

- Think of questions you'd most likely be asked by reporters and practice your answers.

- Develop a standard set of "message points" about your group, organization or company. Have them handy or have them memorized.

- Set up a mock news conference and have staff ask you questions.

- Videotape your mock press conferences to see how you performed. Ask staff members to watch the video replay with you and offer brutally honest critiques.

- Take your practicing seriously by watching how others handle the task. Watch televised news conferences to see how interview subjects are handling the questions and the pressure.

- Practice and plan.

These are just some of the very, very basics. There's a lot more to spokesperson training. It is one of those things you will get good at with time and practice.

Remember, there is power in preparation. Remember, you are preparing in the event of a crisis. The better prepared you are – or your spokesperson is – the better your group, organization or company will look when the press comes calling.

So who is your spokesperson? List the people within your group/organization and their strong points which would make them good spokespeople. People you will put to work, as you will see in the next section.

Please read on.

TIM HERRERA

Speak clearly, if you speak at all; carve every
word before you let it fall.
-Oliver Wendell Holmes, Sr.

TIM HERRERA

Put your spokesperson to work

We've already been over this, so hopefully you have hand-picked a person or two who will serve as the primary spokespeople to represent your company or organization. Inform everyone who answers a phone that if a call comes in from the media that they s should direct any media inquiries to the spokesperson or spokespeople. Be firm in telling staffers that they are NOT TO ANSWER REPORTER'S QUESTIONS. You want to make sure that you are speaking with a united voice and that you have specific spokespeople.

Your spokespeople could find themselves under a great deal of pressure, the kind they have never experienced before. So, make sure during times of crisis that they have no other duties to worry about so that they can concentrate on the crisis at hand. Give them space and give them support. They will need it. If you are the spokesperson, you will need that help and support.

While communicating with the media during a crisis, the designated spokesperson must:

-Demonstrate that the entire organization is concerned about the people involved.

-Explain what is being done to fix the situation. Explain in detail the steps that you are taking. Make a list. Remember: lists can be your friend.

- Keep the message consistent with all interested parties. Never tell one group anything that is not being told to the media.

- Be open, honest, and tell YOUR full story, to the extent that it is possible. If you do not, someone else will. That's not a risk you want to take. Not being open and honest increases the odds that the crisis team could lose control of the situation.

- Never respond with "no comment." Instead explain why you cannot answer the question. For example, you do not have those all of the details confirmed at this time, or you will provide the media with an update when you do have the answer to a particular question. Start out by saying something like "We cannot comment at this time because..." And then offer several reasons for your actions.

- Don't guess about anything. If you don't know the answer, just say so and tell those questioning you that you will find the answer and get back to them if possible. Just make sure that you keep this promise.

- Respect reporter deadlines. If you promise to get information, do so as quickly as possible. Respecting reporters' deadlines will reduce the chances that they will be badgering you just when you need that the least.

- Never speak off the record. The media can use any information released. Even if you feel you can speak in confidence to a reporter you might still find that information being reported.

- Never give exclusive interviews during a crisis. All members of the media should have the chance for gathering information. You have to play fair. Playing favorites will come back to haunt you!

CRISIS COMMUNICATION PLANNING

-If an injury or death has occurred, do not release the name(s) of the injured/deceased until next of kin (immediate family) have been notified. The last thing a family member wants to do is learn about a horrible incident involving a loved one while watching the evening news. Place yourselves in their shoes.

-Do not discuss who is "responsible for the incident", or who is "legally liable" in any way. These types of things have the potential of getting you in more trouble.

-Do not discuss illegal activity. Refer all questions to the appropriate law enforcement agency. It is okay to say things like "Police are investigating. We are cooperating." That's the safest approach.

-Be available. Provide reporters with a cell phone number where they can contact you. You must be accessible to them during a crisis. You want the information going to the press to come from you as the "source."

-Notify receptionists and other employees to direct all media inquiries to the designated spokesperson without speculating on the situation to whoever is calling. A reporter is just doing his/her job and might ask questions of anyone who answers the phone. Besides, the people taking the initial calls are not the spokespeople and they likely don't have all the facts.

-In cases when the media request interviews with family members, offer to provide someone who can act as a liaison to family members for the media so that the family can protect their privacy if that's what they want. However, make sure the media realizes that this person should **not** be considered the "family spokesperson" unless that's what the family wants.

-Avoid "side comments" meant to be humorous. A crisis isn't the time to entertain. Comments can often be taken out of context. In many cases they are taken out of context or misunderstood.

-Do NOT respond to hypothetical questions. These types of things also can be taken out of context and stretched beyond belief.

-Use everyday language, not jargon that is specific to your line of work, when talking to reporters. Make the situation as easy to understand as possible. Using job slang or acronyms may not only confuse listeners but they slow things down and are distracting. People at home watching TV or listening to the radio will say to themselves "What did he say?" and they will miss out on important information.

-Provide written materials that give reporters background information. Keep stacks of program brochures or fact sheets handy in case you need them. If you don't have anything like that available it's okay to print information from your website. In most cases, if the media is responding to a fast-breaking crisis there was no time to print information off the Internet before they left the office.

    This is an extensive list, but if you follow each point you will find that it is easier for your – or your designated spokesperson – to deal with the challenging task of speaking with the media. Speaking with the media during an ongoing crisis is tough and even the most seasoned people struggle at times because so much is happening all at once. The above list will help get you through that challenge.

A spokesperson should not go into an interview situation empty handed. In fact, he or she should have in his or her hand a list of message points to get across when addressing the media. What are message points, you ask? Read on to the next section where we will be discussing that very topic!

TIM HERRERA

Good words are worth much, and cost little.
-George Herbert

TIM HERRERA

Develop key messages

You've chosen someone as your spokesperson during a crisis. That's great. Now, what is that person going to say? What are the key messages to deliver?

Key messages during a crisis are different compared to any other time of business, but the concept is fundamentally the same. Just think about what it is that you want to say publicly and say it.

A word of caution here: there are times when there are some things that you just can't talk about for legal reasons. Remember, we mentioned that earlier. Maybe there's litigation involved or it's a sensitive legal matter. During these times, consider consulting your attorney – if you have one – to go over things that you cannot and should not say publicly.

Now we are going to discuss what you are going to say and how you are going to say it. It has taken a while to reach this point but it was important that we went over all of the other information first.

It's important that you spend time figuring out your key messages. These are three to five sentences or phrases that you really want to drive home. While it is likely that you will want to relay a lot of information, there are key points you will want to make clear to the media during crisis situations.

With your interview or news conference approaching, you can't just wing it. You need prepared messages. You need the types of messages that make your point and express your position, or your organization's position on an issue.

Key messages are also often called talking points or message points. You will use them to communicate with your target audience during interviews or news conferences. Remember that while you are responding to questions from an interviewer or group of interviewers, you also are reaching out to an audience. You want that audience to know you are in control of the crisis situation. These messages are important to have, important to keep, and vitally important to commit to memory.

Key messages are an integral part of your communication effort. When developing and using message points, you have to make sure that what you are saying is clear and understandable. You don't want anything that you say to create mixed messages, or sound as if they have double meaning. In most cases, straight talk should produce straight results.

Preparation is vital. There are a lot of things to consider when preparing your messages. First, you have to consider what the important points are that you need to make during this crisis confronting you.

If you are preparing for a news conference – or a one-on-one interview - narrow down a short list of relevant points that you want to share. And in this case, in any case, think in terms of using bullet points instead of paragraphs. Bullet points are easier to read and follow rather than trying to keep your place while reading paragraphs.

CRISIS COMMUNICATION PLANNING

Here are some things to take into account when developing messages and message points:

-Be concise and to the point. Long responses are not good responses.

-Try to keep your list of messages to between three and five key points. If you go beyond five points, you risk losing your listener who is trying to focus on what you are saying.

-Try to accentuate the positive and de-emphasize the negative. You want to remain upbeat if you can, depending on the topic of the interview.

-Make your messages consistent. They need to fit together like puzzle pieces. Conflicting messages send mixed messages.

-Stay focused on the interviewer as much as possible. Glance at your notes to help stay on-topic, but try to maintain eye contact with those doing the questioning.

-Be deliberate with your messages. They all must have a point.

-Make your messages simple and easy to remember.

-Use simple words and language when possible. Sometimes, we do have to use specific words and terminology, but speak as plainly as possible.

-Be honest, believable and credible.

You will find the above list helping in developing message points when either facing a crisis situation or you are garden variety news conference or media interview.

Sometimes people are able to memorize the messages they are using, but you must make sure that what you are saying does not sound too rehearsed. You don't want to seem robotic.

In many cases, it works just as well to concentrate on using key words and phrases that can help you make your point.

A lot goes into message development. You will find plenty of books and helpful articles on this subject. Refer to them if you feel the need, but what key message development really boils down to is this: What are the main things you want the people – the public, your stakeholders - to come away with after you are done speaking and/or answering questions? What do you want people to remember most as you are handling this crisis? Figure that out and you've nailed it.

Figure out what your spokespeople are going to say and how they are going to say it. Write it down and practice it. Stick to the message. Keep repeating the key points that you want to make and do your best to communicate with confidence.

In our next section, we will discuss the media avenues to pursue when delivering your message during a crisis. There are plenty of them.

Whatever words we utter should be chosen with care for people will hear them and be influenced by them for good or ill.
-Buddha

TIM HERRERA

Determine the best channels of communications

When something bad happens, you need to start telling people connected with your organization. And, obviously, you need to do that before you reach out to the media or the media contacts you. I am talking about interested parties both on the inside and the outside. But what is the best way to reach stakeholders with the information? What's the best way to approach the dissemination of information?

Start internally first with the people who work for or with you. Sometimes these folks are referred to as **internal stakeholders**. If there's something big happening, these people not only have a right to know; they have a need to know.

If some crisis is underway – and it's not immediately apparent to staff – let people within your organization know what's going on.

First, you should consider calling an emergency staff meeting to start informing others. Tell everyone there the truth, or as much truth as you are able to unveil depending on the situation. It is important for you to stamp out any potential rumors from the very beginning; otherwise, there's no telling what kind of information could reach the public.

If your organization is large and spread out, in addition to calling a staff meeting, you should send out an electronic memo to all employees explaining the current situation. You don't have to go into great detail. Just provide enough information – the RIGHT information – to inform your people as to what's happening and how it could impact them and your organization. Remember that you are not doing this to alarm people; you are doing this to inform people.

There are several ways in which you can communicate to people within your organization regarding a developing crisis situation:

-Group Email

-Internal memo

-Staff meeting

-Voice mail message

-Conference call

-Video message posted on your intranet or sent via email

If your work situation involves some sort of Board or other similar structure then it would be best to take the time to make some individual phone calls. This will give you an opportunity to calmly address the matter, explain your approach, and even entertain suggestions in dealing with your situation.

In your communication with employees and co-workers remember to let them know that in the event your crisis situation attracts news coverage they should refer all media inquiries to you, your designee or your appointed spokesperson.

If you are facing a crisis situation and you need people to pitch in to help deal with all aspects of a calamity, then start assigning staff members into various teams to handle specific jobs. We will address that in more detail in a later section.

Now that you've dealt with internal matters and informed people "on the inside" as to what is going on, now it's time to look externally. How are you going to publicly respond? Will it be through a news release, a news conference, or by conducting individual interviews with reporters?

If you are really getting inundated with interview requests, and the incident is an ongoing one, consider holding periodic news conferences to stay in touch with reporters and to make sure you can quash any rumors that begin to percolate.

The fastest way to communicate may be through your local news radio stations. If a crisis breaks involving your organization, consider contacting the news radio stations in your town and offering to have your spokespeople interviewed "live on the air" to tell the public what's happening.

As you prepare to reach out "externally" you have to take into consideration what you are going to say, how much you are going to say, and for how long you are going to say it. One thing you want to avoid is being forced to speculate and offer conjecture. You should only talk about what you know.

If you are quickly planning a news conference to address your crisis, your best approach is to distribute a media advisory which announces to the press that you are going to have an event. In this case, it is a news conference. The advisory is a bare bones announcement with a bare amount of facts. Below is a sample that you can use:

SAMPLE MEDIA ADVISORY

Media Advisory

Put the main headline here

The Sub-Headline Goes Here and It Includes Additional Information in Italics

CITY OR COMPANY NAME CAN GO HERE – This is where you write a brief paragraph or two to tell the editors why you are holding a news conference. Remember, this is not a press release where you have to pack in a bunch of facts. You can just include the basics to advise people about the upcoming news conference, its purpose, who will be there and at what time.

Unlike a press release, you don't have to write "For Immediate Release" on advisories because you are just giving the media a "heads up" about something down the road. Editors often put media advisories in their files for future reference. However, in this case it is for an event that is happening very soon.

WHO: Explain who will be attending

CRISIS COMMUNICATION PLANNING

WHAT: News Conference (this is a good place to offer more facts if you have them)

WHERE: Give the exact location down to the zip code and room number of your event

WHEN: Day, Date, Time

This would be a good place to provide editors with the names of all the individuals associated with your group or organization who will be available for individual interviews before, during, or after your news conference.

Contact:

Your Name
Your Title
Your Company/Group/Organization
Your phone numbers both desk and cell
Your e-mail address
Your web site – if you have one

About You

This where you will put a little background information about your company/group/organization. Keep it to a brief, one-paragraph description of who you are and what you do. Remember that since this is a crisis situation and something bad has happened, so this is not a promotional item.

Don't forget to include the media advisory on your Web site if there is an appropriate place there.

Eventually, you will need to write a news release to inform your employees, other stakeholders and the general public about the crisis and describe how you and your organization are responding. A news release has much more detail than a media advisory. They are designed to be more informative.

SAMPLE NEWS RELEASE

FOR IMMEDIATE RELEASE:

CONTACT:
Your Name
Your Company's Name
Phone Number/Cell Number
FAX Number
Email Address
Website Address

Headline for your announcement

Your headline must get the editor's attention. Since this is a crisis situation, then it should. Write is in bold type with a font that is larger than the body text. Preferred type fonts are Arial, Times New Roman, or Verdana. Keep the headline brief and capitalize every word with the exception of "a", "the" "an" or any word that is three characters or less.

CRISIS COMMUNICATION PLANNING

<City>, <State>, <Date> - The first paragraph of your release should be written in a clear and concise manner. The opening sentence contains the most important information; keep it to 25 words or less. Never take for granted that the reader has read your headline. It needs contain information that will inform the reader. Remember, you are dealing with a crisis and must only deal with facts. This is not the time to promote a product.

Don't forget to answer "who", "what", "when", "where", "why" and "how". Your text should include relevant information about the situation. Make sure to include pertinent details based on what you have determined reporters will ask.

If you're writing to announce a news conference, include the date, location, and any other pertinent information.

Keep your sentences and paragraphs short; a paragraph should be no more than 3-4 sentences. Your release should be brief, between 500 to 800 words, written in a word processing program, and spell checked for errors.

Watch for grammatical errors. Proofread! The mood of the release should be factual. Don't hype anything.

The last paragraph before the company information should read: For additional information on (put in the subject of this release), contact "name" or visit www.yoururl.com. If you have boilerplate information about products and services now is the time to remove that language because now is not the time to make sales pitches.

ABOUT <COMPANY> - Include a brief description of your company, without making it seem like a promotional announcement.

- END – or - ###

At the end of the release, you need to indicate that the release is ended. This lets the journalists know they have received the entire release. Type "End" or type "###" on the first line after your text is completed. If your release goes over one page, type "MORE" at the bottom of the first page.

You can distribute news releases during and after your crisis. They are excellent tools to inform people of how you are dealing with your current situation. Use them sparingly. One announcement per day, depending on the length of your crisis, should be sufficient. Remember that you will likely be holding news conferences as well. So, you will be informing people in both written and verbal form.

It takes a while to get the knack for writing media advisories and news releases. If you have a trained person within your organization who can do this, you are in good shape. If you don't have someone in-house who can write these announcements for you, it might be a good idea to consider hiring a professional, if you can. Otherwise, this is a skill that you can learn.

    And that is what we will discuss in our next section. See you there!

Communication - the human connection - is the key to personal and career success.
-Paul J. Meyer

TIM HERRERA

Stick with what you know and be honest

If you are old enough you remember there once was an old police television drama called *Dragnet*. One of the main characters was the no-nonsense Sgt. Joe Friday and one of his favorite phrases when conducting interviews with victims and witnesses was "Just the facts, please."

Basically, what Joe was always trying to tell people was just tell what you know. Just the facts. Offer no speculation. Speculation can get you into hot water. That is how you should approach speaking to anyone during a crisis, whether it is with an internal stakeholder or a member of the media.

You don't want to relay information to people if you are not 100-percent certain that information is true and accurate. Remember that an acceptable answer to a question for which you don't know the answer is "I don't know." However, you can say that in different ways without sounding uniformed. You can say, "I don't know the answer to that but I will get back to you as soon as I can." Or you can say, "I don't have that information right now but if it is something we can comment on or release we will do so later."

You don't want to find yourself in trouble for relaying "facts" that were not really facts.

If a reporter is asking you about the circumstances surrounding a crisis tell that reporter only what you know. Do not hypothesize because that can lead to more conjecture and more rumors.

The same goes for when you are speaking with someone from your Board of Directors, or someone on that level. Just report what you know to be true. Speculation will do you more harm than good.

And when sticking to the facts, remember that you also need to be honest and open with your comments.

Another important thing to remember when dealing with the media at any time – whether during a crisis or a normal situation – that you MUST avoid saying **"no comment."**

Just let me say briefly here that saying "no comment" is the last thing you want to say to a reporter because it will only prompt that person to dig deeper or go elsewhere for facts. Remember that you want to be in control of the facts, or I should say, you want to be in control of your information.

There are ways of answering questions without providing information that you are either not prepared or not allowed to release. You are not trying to be evasive, but you are trying to make sure that you don't say the wrong thing at the wrong time.

It is important that you be truthful with reporters at all times – or at least as truthful as you can possibly be – because lies and misconceptions have a nasty way of coming back to bite you. Once reporters have learned the real extent of the problem, and they realize you told them something completely different, they will automatically stop trusting you. They will even accuse you of trying to deceive them. Never, ever say anything to a reporter that you know is **not true**. If you do that you will lose your credibility **instantly**.

So, if you are ever questioned by a reporter, or you have to relay some important information to a stakeholder during a crisis situation, just pretend that you are the gruff, yet truthful, Sgt. Friday and just stick to the facts, please.

When a crisis erupts, you will likely find yourself facing a lot of different tasks all at the same time. This is when you have to rely on some of the people around you to help carry the load. That is what we will discuss in our next section, sharing communication duties during a crisis.

# TIM HERRERA

In a crisis, don't hide behind anything or anybody.
They're going to find you anyway.
-Paul Bryant

TIM HERRERA

Commutations duties during a crisis

If you find yourself in the middle of a crisis, one of the first things you will realize is that you have a lot of things to do while a lot of things are happening around you. However, if there are other members on your team, you don't have to do everything by yourself.

In this section, we will discuss the different types of help you will need during a crisis situation, especially one involving the media.

In the event of a crisis your designated communications person will have to...

-Determine if an official statement should be prepared and released to the press and the general public.

-With the help of assigned team members, prepare the message.

-Talk with all personnel who are assigned to answer the phone directing them to send all media inquiries to the designated communications person, or those assigned to assist that person.

-Look over and discuss the prepared statement prior to distribution when possible because you don't want to exclude important information, or include something unnecessary.

- Coordinate distribution of information through the media, website, publications and even direct mail.

- Figure out the best way of sending out a statement to all interested parties. (E-mail? Fax? Text message?)

- Designate someone who will coordinate information gathering from outside authorities.

As you can tell, those are far too many duties for one person to tackle. Delegate these duties to different people. This is not something you should take on alone.

In the event of a crisis, on-going response is crucial. So here are some other important duties to consider. These are duties that you can take on alone, but should consider farming out to other members of your team:

- Assign someone to update all interested parties about changes to or additional details of the situation by some of all of the following methods: voice mail, e-mail, faxes, information hotline, press conferences, media contacts, phone contact, assemblies, letters, newsletters/other publications.

- Figure out how often you should send out updates based upon availability of facts and other factors, like availability of those assigned to speak.

- Pick someone to collect and circulate information until things have returned to the way they were before the crisis.

CRISIS COMMUNICATION PLANNING

-Select someone to pay attention to the media coverage of the situation. That person will have to contact media outlets and quickly correct any reported misinformation. Sometimes the right information you distributed is reported incorrectly. You don't want wrong information floating around out there.

-When the crisis is over and things are more normal, assess the success of your plan and make changes as necessary.

There are likely even more communication duties during a crisis but the ones listed above should be at the heart of your focus. The important thing to remember is that you cannot and should not try to handle every aspect of crisis communication by yourself. It's all too much for one person.

As we have mentioned, when a crisis hits you have to start letting people know what has happened and how you are responding to the situation. But who is on that list of people that must be contacted? How do you determine who needs to be contacted and who does not?

In our next section, we will discuss narrowing down your list of stakeholders, or interested parties as they are sometimes called.

TIM HERRERA

Successful people recognize crisis as a time for change - from lesser to greater, smaller to bigger.
-Edwin Louis Cole

TIM HERRERA

Who are your interested parties?

When a crisis hits, do you think you will have time to run through a mental list of people to contact? I think we both know the answer to that question. So, in this section the goal is to learn how to develop of list of stakeholders or interested parties to contact in the event of a crisis situation.

There are two types of interested parties that you will be dealing with during a crisis situation. They are the "internal" and "external" interested parties and they are broken down into sub-groups. Depending on your situation, your interested parties might be made up of more than the sub-groups mentioned below.

Internal
-Employees
-Visitors
-Volunteers
-Board of Directors (if you have them)
-Board Members (if you have them)

The people that you put on the above list (the list you WILL make) are the easiest to contact. When you create your list, make sure you have all of the necessary contact information available for all of these people.

You will need work phone numbers, home phone numbers, cell phone numbers, email addresses, and home addresses. There is no telling which might be the best way to connect with these people, so have every possible communication option available on your list.

Once you have started spreading your information internally, you have to think about externally too. You will find there are many, many people outside of your organization who also might be impacted by the crisis you are experiencing.

Below is a list of some of the external interested parties you will have to contact, or communicate with during a crisis situation:

External

-Neighboring business or neighbors

-Families of Employees

-Families of Visitors

-Media - Print and Electronic

-Local Community-At-Large

-Clients

Depending on your individual situation, you may have more groups to add to these lists.

Please list them so that you know who you might have to contact in the event that you are involved in a crisis. You don't want to leave anyone out! If things start getting really busy you might end up unintentionally leaving someone out of the loop.

It's really a good idea to have these kinds of lists written down ahead of time. Create your lists and put them in a safe place, like a binder, so you can have easy access to the contact information you need.

I have found that one of the best ways to deal with tough situations – or even not so touch ones – is to work off of checklists. Checklists are really helping in making sure we've assigned all the necessary duties and completed all of the important tasks.

In our next section, we will look at a sample checklist that you might find helpful someday.

TIM HERRERA

Never waste a crisis.
-Mark Rutte

TIM HERRERA

Immediate response duties checklist

If you have a designated Incident Management Team, that group will oversee the completion of the steps listed below. If you don't have such a team, I strongly urge you to establish one. During a crisis, various tasks will be assigned by your organization's president, CEO, or designated spokesperson depending on the situation needing attention. An Incident Management Team will prove to be invaluable to you.

It is likely that in the event of a crisis, employees will be recruited to help with implementing the crisis communications plan and other related duties. During emergencies, people from your various departments may be assigned to assist the designated spokesperson and Incident Management Team.

Here are some steps to check:

Step One - First Alert

-Notify supervisors and designated spokesperson.

-Ask the switchboard to send all media calls to the designated spokesperson.

-Try to evaluate the situation and level of impact.

-Decide whether to issue a written media statement or to hold a press briefing.

-Pick a location for press briefings, the more accessible the better.

-Notify the media to the time and location of press briefing. Also let the switchboard know in case the press asks about the briefing.

Step Two - Gathering the Facts

-Put together a list of facts. No rumors. Just the facts.

-Check with the proper authorities to confirm what's going on.

-Determine if there are injuries and/or fatalities but do not release the names. Leave that up to the proper authorities.

-Evaluate the potential for public health risk, if the possibility exists.

-Determine what authorities (police, fire, etc.) you must and should consult.

-Talk with responding agencies to coordinate the release of the information you are giving out to the press and the public.

-Start working on the message that you will release to media and the general public. Make sure that you use the key messages worksheet that you have already created because you've been following all the suggestions in this book.

-Begin notifying internal stakeholder audiences from the list that you've already created. You want people in the "inside" learning the facts before they are released to those on the "outside."

Step Three - Verify and Keep the Information Moving

CRISIS COMMUNICATION PLANNING

-Keep written records of the exact times that specific information arrives. You need to record what information is the most recent to make sure that old information does not get released to the press.

-Make sure your facts are straight before you release them. Check with the assisting agencies and with teammates you are working with to make sure that you are all on the same page.

-Keep all of the appropriate interested parties updated on what's going on and do that on a fairly regular basis. "Fairly regular" is something you can determine later.

-Stay in touch with the appropriate government and legal authorities so that they know exactly what's happening.

Step Four - Prepare for Media (Calls and Visits)

-Create a "media contact record" so that you know who has contacted you and when. Sometimes the same media outlets will assign more than one reporter to a story. Keeping a contact record will allow you to say "I've already given that information to someone from your organization. Please check with them."

-Put your designated media spokesperson through a brief rehearsal. Go through your "What information media will want" list and rehearse what verified information you plan on making available to the press and the public.

-Discuss how you're going to alert the media. Will it be through press conferences? Written releases? Faxes? All of the above?

-Start getting your pre-arranged media room/ work area ready. This room will be either on or off site. If necessary, establish a work space for reporters to gather the information you'll give them.

-Make sure that before you release any information that you get the approval for your media statement, handout or press release from your president, CEO or manager.

-Pick those officials or team members who will read statements or speak during press conferences or with reporters during interviews.

-Make sure that everyone within your organization understands your group's guidelines for dealing with the media. You all have to work as a team. You can't afford to have people "striking out on their own."

Step Five - Get Ready for Reporters to Arrive

-Don't be afraid to ask those folks who say that they are members of the media for identification and ask them to sign in. ALL reporters should carry some kind of press badge or other form of identification. They should be able to provide something more than a business card.

-Inform the reporters of the restrictions on movement, photography, and videotaping.

Stay calm, take a few breaths and start your press briefing.

-Make sure that you advise media of the time and place of the next and future updates. It will cut down on the number of calls you'll receive requesting information. Reporters will also like the fact that you are thinking ahead.

-Remember to follow-up on additional media inquiries and keep any promises that you've made with reporters to "get back to them" if you've been asked a question that you don't have the answer to at the time. However, in those follow-up calls don't reveal new information that you wouldn't give out to everyone else.

Step Six - Media Follow-up & On-going Relations

-Watch, listen to and read the media coverage to make sure that what's being reported about what's going on is accurate.

-Ask media outlets for corrections of factual errors, if necessary. You have to set the record straight immediately if reporting mistakes have been made. Just make sure that you are asking in a firm, yet polite manner. Remember that during crises that reporters are under stress too.

-Inform the media of any significant new developments as they happen. You want to be in charge of distributing the information. Basically, you want to tell them about any changes. You don't want them telling you.

-Keep a record of all media contact so that you know which media outlets you are dealing with. This will also help you in your efforts to follow-up and monitor what's being reported.

-Assess the effectiveness of your crisis communications plan and make the appropriate changes as you see fit.

Now, that is quite a list and there are quite a few steps. But I think if you use the above list as a guide, or use it to create a list of your own, you will find it to be a useful tool during a crisis situation. Remember, there will be so many things going on at the time that you will never be able to remember everything. That is why it's important to work from lists.

When that crisis does hit, you'll find that the media will be hitting you with a lot of questions. But what types of questions? What will reporters ask? Let's focus on that in our next section.

Crisis and pressure help foster change - that's why I'm not so pessimistic towards crises.
-Wolfgang Schauble

TIM HERRERA

What the media will ask about during crisis situations

During a breaking news or crisis situation, you will be hit with a lot of questions from reporters. Some of these questions will seem to be very intrusive, or even insensitive. In your wildest dreams you will have never anticipated what some of those questions might be. Below is a list of possible things you could be asked by reporters, as well as your internal and external interested parties.

Remember: information about PEOPLE should always come first. Information about property should follow. Use this list as a guide to prepare your answers needed during a crisis situation:

Casualties

-Number killed or injured or who escaped (use caution with initial numbers and remember to emphasize the numbers are subject to change as the situation evolves).

-Nature of injuries.

-Care given to the people who have been injured.

-The celebrity of anyone, who may have been killed, injured or escaped.

Property Damage

-Estimated value of loss. (Be very careful with estimate numbers because they often change rapidly!)

-Description of property.

-Importance of the property.

-Other property threatened.

-Insurance protection. (Reporters will always ask: Were you insured?)

Causes

-Statements from participants.

-Statements from witnesses.

-Statements from key responders, such as members of your crisis management team, local police and fire department.

How emergency was discovered

-Who was the first to make the report and to whom did they report?

-Who sounded the alarm and alerted the authorities?

-Who called for help, and how quickly that was done?

Rescue and Relief

-The number of people involved in the rescue and relief efforts.

-The names of any prominent people or groups helping.

-The type of rescue equipment being used.

-Any physically disabled persons needing to be rescued.

-How the emergency was prevented from spreading.

-How property was saved.

-Any people you want to thank for pitching in and helping with relief efforts.

Details of the emergency

-Description of the crisis.

-Attempts at escape or rescue.

-Length of time it might take before emergency is over.

-Loss of structures and/or other property.

Incidentals

-Number of spectators, how spectators reacted and crowd control.

-Unusual happenings involved with the emergency.

-State of mind, concerns, or stress of families and survivors. (Be careful: you can't really "speak for someone else" unless you have been designated to do so.)

Legal actions

-Inquests, coroner's reports.

-Police follow-up.

-Insurance company actions.

-Professional negligence or inaction.

-Suits stemming from the incident.

Caution: be extremely careful when handling questions involving legal actions. It's best to NOT address them, if possible. Many times reporters are looking ahead "beyond the crisis" and trying to determine if anyone will be seeking damages. It's really important to steer clear of this.

If you are ever asked a question, during a crisis about whether you plan on suing, or you anticipate being sued, the best response is something like this: "We don't believe that this is the time of place to discuss something like that."

Now, as you look back at the above list I know it seems overwhelming. But keep in mind that those are the types of things reporters will want to know. In fact, those are the types of things that both your internal and external "interested parties" will want to know.

Just be prepared. Don't be surprised if you are asked these types of questions. The good thing to remember here is that you will be prepared, and not surprised, by these types of questions.

This book is all about preparation and planning. In our next section, we did deeper into the delegation of duties process which will make it easier to execute your well-developed plan.

The crisis of today is the joke of tomorrow.
-H. G. Wells

TIM HERRERA

Crisis Meeting Agenda

During your initial internal briefing about the crisis, you will need to gather some very specific information. You will also have to delegate certain jobs in order to help things run as smoothly as possible. And you have to keep track of who is doing what job.

The following specific agenda items that you should review:

Situation report:

-What happened and what appears to be the cause?

-Gather confirmed facts, such as establishing a chronology of events, determining the consequences, or possible consequences, as you know them.

-Figure out the scale of the proposed situation. In other words, how bad things are at the moment.

Initial response status:

-What is being done?

-Who is doing what, and why?

-What are you doing and is it enough?

-When will you begin responding and how long will it take?

Initial communications status:

-Who knows what's going on, who needs to know immediately and later on.

-Let the switchboard know that you will start getting phone calls and have them direct the calls to the right people.

Short-term response requirements:

-Farm out crisis communications responsibilities to team members.

-Figure out what must be done immediately and in the next several hours.

-Figure out what human and material resources are available or needed.

Short-term communication process:

-Staff, faculty, students, families, etc.

Next meeting time.

-Set up your next meeting time and establish information deadlines. Make it clear to your team members that if you've asked them to gather specific information that you need that information by your next meeting. Think of it this way: reporters have deadlines and so do you.

All of this can be extremely overwhelming, especially for someone with no media experience. At some point, if the burden gets to be too much, you might want to consider hiring a professional communications person to help ease your burden. And that is the topic we will explore in our next section.

In prehistoric times, mankind often had only two choices in crisis situations: fight or flee. In modern times, humor offers us a third alternative; fight, flee - or laugh.

-Robert Orben

TIM HERRERA

Professional help or do-it-yourself?

So, a big question remains: Should you hire a full-time communications specialist? The answer: that depends...

Many companies, organizations and groups wrestle with the question of whether to have a full-time communications specialist on staff. There are many pros and cons to consider when making this decision.

Let's go over the cons first, not because I am a negative person but because I want to get them out of the way, and because I am MORE in favor of companies having full-time media people than not. That is, of course, if hiring a communications person is a financial option for you or your organization.

Having someone on staff dedicated solely to doing media related work is worth considering; however, do you have room in the budget to make the kind of financial commitment necessary when hiring a full-time media professional? The position would cost a small company, or any company for that matter, a good chunk of money. Make sure there's enough money in your bucket before taking the leap.

Are you really going to be doing enough media outreach project possibilities to justify having a communications director or some other kind of media specialist working for you all the time? If there are not enough projects being planned or produced then you are under-employing someone and over-extending your spending.

What kind of impact will it have on your tiny, multi-tasking staff if you have one person doing only one job? Many small – and even medium sized organizations – employ people who wear many hats and perform many duties. You might have a hard time justifying the position to other staff members – and even yourself – especially if the media person does not produce stellar results, if any results at all.

Ask yourself if you are only hiring a full-time media person in order to brag about it at the local chamber of commerce brown bag luncheons every Tuesday afternoon? If you are trying to give the illusion to your business friends and competitors that you can "play ball with the big boys" then you had better think long and hard about your decision. If this is your justification then you are making a mistake.

Many medium sized businesses and organizations have full-time media relations or public relations people on staff, and they work very hard because they are usually a one-person operation. Small companies rarely have an employee solely dedicated to media. It's usually not something that fits into the budget. You have to decide for yourself what's right for you and your organization.

Now, let's look at the pro side of the pro/con list regarding the debate over keeping a full-time communications person on staff. Here are some good reasons why it's worth considering:

-A full-time communications professional can contribute to the development of your organization's overall strategic plan, especially if that plan includes a facet of media relations – and hopefully it does.

-If you have a strategic plan – and let's hope you do – the communications professional can help support you in enacting your plan and assist in explaining the plan to employees or staff members.

-Since all groups, organizations and companies have specific interests a full-time communications staffer can develop policies, procedures and materials to help you "tell your story".

-You will get a better fix on the "pulse of the local community" by having a person on the job dedicated to doing just that.

-Having an employee solely focused on getting your group or organization's name "out there" improves those chances. It also saves high level employees from having to worry about media matters while still keeping the place running.

-Having a communications person on staff provides you with someone who can represent the organization out in the community, who can take all calls from the press, and who can concentrate on trying to get media outlets to report news stories about your company, group or organization.

Again, this argument boils down to money. I know it sounds like I am being repetitive, redundant and repetitive. However, if you have the money to keep somebody on full-time to deal with the media, then go ahead and do so.

If you can't justify a full-time hire then consider hiring someone on a part-time contract. There are plenty of good media relations firms out there who will take you on as a project and they will do good work.

Most likely, you probably don't have the budgetary room for a hire like this of any kind, and that's why you bought this book.

It is possible for small and medium sized companies, organizations and nonprofits, to handle media relations fairly well without having a communications director or media relations manager on staff. Just remember that it's an investment in time and effort to do things correctly.

There are some great communications companies out there who specialize in crisis management. If you have the means to contract with one to help you through a crisis involving the media, then do it. These folks are out there and they are ready to rock, if you need them.

Here is another list of things to remember when it comes to crisis communications planning:

-It's better to over-estimate the crisis than to under-estimate it. By over-estimating you will be able to use all the tools that you have in place to solve your problems quickly.

-When you are talking to the media about the crisis at hand remember the order of importance of your concerns: people always come first, property always second, and money is third. You know in your heart that's right any way, but it's important that you remember that sequence, otherwise you could be labeled as cold and callous.

-If the crisis was somehow preventable, you have to prepare a response to the question **"how can you prevent this from happening again?"** In fact, when you are crafting your message points, that's something to include. Make sure that your answers are also "solution oriented." Have your solutions ready.

-Monitor the coverage in progress for accuracy. If reporters are making mistakes pull them aside, kindly and politely, and tell them. You need reporters to disseminate your message and they need you as a source of information.

-It's important for you to understand that underestimating the extent of a crisis can be costly, just ask British Petroleum (BP) Oil about the underwater leak in the Gulf of Mexico. That was a classic case of underestimating a crisis.

When a crisis hits what happens within the first few hours is crucial. Whatever the media reports sets the tone for the event, so the first impression that the media gets from you is extremely important. It's better to be proactive than reactive, so please plan ahead. Someday you'll get glad that you did.

Of course, this is just a thumbnail sketch of media crisis planning and it barely scratches the surface. There are many, many fine books out there that offer much greater detail about crisis communications planning. And, again, there are also many fine firms out there specializing in this area.

If you really feel that your company or organization could use some professional help in this area, then contact one of those companies to see how much it would cost for them to conduct a one or two-day seminar for you and your staff. In the end, it could be money well spent. If you don't have the money for something like that then I hope this chapter has been or will be helpful to you.

As you might have noticed, this book (meaning the author) is big on using lists. In our next section, we will go over one final list that will help you in your crisis media planning.

Please read on.

Real style is not having a program - it's how one behaves in a crisis.
-Frank Auerbach

TIM HERRERA

Crisis Management Checklist

During a crisis, it is really important that you assess your needs. At any time, it is also important that you assess your overall communication needs. As you begin working on your plans, consider the following points important aspects to consider during the plan creation process.

-Did you develop a plan in advance for a crisis?

-Did you put together a crisis management team that you can call into action quickly?

-What are your media objectives?

-Is your spokesperson springing into action?

-Did you craft key messages?

-Have you determined the best channels of communications to use during this crisis?

-Are you sticking with what you know?

-Are you being honest and open with reporters and avoiding saying "no comment"?

-Are you being honest with yourself and determining if you need professional communications help?

Each crisis can be considered unique in nature and might require slightly different responses, depending on the situation. However, it is really important that you have some type of plan in place to handle both internal and external communications matters.

I hope that you will consider this book a guide for you in the event that you are facing a crisis that might involve the media. Crisis media planning or crisis communications is different from other types of communications efforts. Hopefully, you will never be faced with such a situation.

However, as I've mentioned throughout this book, if you are able to hire professional communications help you should do so, especially in the event of a crisis. Crisis communications really is a specialty and some people who focus on that for a living are really worth their price. But if you don't have the money to hire specialists then hopefully you will find this book helpful.

Crises refine life. In them you discover what you are.
-Allan K. Chalmers

TIM HERRERA

Relax

One final word: relax.

Can you believe that I'm telling you to relax? The nerve of me! It's easier said than done, but the truth is that you really need to calm down as much as possible during a crisis situation so that you can see things more clearly and think more clearly.

Take a moment or two to breathe deeply. Lie down if you have to. Do whatever you have to do to calm yourself down because you know that panicking can only make matters worse.

Be confident in knowing that you have followed the advice laid out in this book. You have developed a good plan. You have put together a great team. You know what to do when dealing with the media during a crisis.

You are ready if that time ever comes.

Good luck, and hang onto this book as your guide.

TIM HERRERA

About the author

Here's some information about me. I am a Communications Director, author, free-lance writer college writing and communications instructor, and a former journalist and radio talk show host.

I worked for 22 years in the journalism business, with most of that time spent honing my public speaking skills in television and radio.

For more than 12 years, I was a reporter and anchor at KCRA-TV in Sacramento where I was fortunate to have earned 14 prestigious journalism awards. I have also worked as a television and radio reporter and anchor in Dallas-Fort Worth and Pittsburgh.

In 2003, I was a runner-up for the Will Rogers Humanitarian Award, presented by the National Society of Newspaper Columnists. I have a B.A. in Journalism from Penn State University and an M.A. in Strategic Communications from National University.

I also have extensive experience in media relations having served as Communications Director for several agencies for the State of California, including the Department of Consumer Affairs and the Department of Conservation.

When I am not working at my communications job or writing books, I teach communication studies courses for colleges that have distance learning programs.

I currently serve as the Communications Director for the Sacramento County Office of Education where I have been fortunate to have earned numerous awards from the California School Public Relations Association (CalSPRA).

For more information visit my Web site: www.timherrera.com.

Thank you!

I want to thank you for taking the time to read this book. It means a lot to me. I believe this book will help you in preparing to deal with the media during a crisis.

I plan on updating this book from time to time. If you have some suggestions for me and would like to suggest a topic, please feel free to send me an email at **timherrera@rocketmail.com**.

I also would appreciate it if you had the time to write a review of this book on Amazon. That will also let me know what additional information readers would like to see in this book.

Best of luck to you!

Tim

TIM HERRERA

Other books by Tim

Media Training: A Guide to Giving Great Interviews

Public Speaking: Simple Steps to Improve Your Skills

What the Online Student MUST Know: Vital Lessons BEFORE Logging On

30 Things You Should Know About Media Relations, 2nd Edition

30 Things You Should Know About Media Relations, 1st Edition

Dad, You Are NOT Going Out Wearing That!

From Wedgies to Feeding Frenzies

Where the Dust Never Settles

I'm Their Dad! Not Their Babysitter!

# TIM HERRERA

Printed in Great Britain
by Amazon